Unbelievable Pictures and Facts About Poland

By: Olivia Greenwood

Introduction

Poland is a very big country, which is filled with lots of history and culture. Today we will be learning all about the very interesting country of Poland.

Do many people come to visit Poland?

Over the years Poland has become quite a popular country to visit. Each year millions of tourists can be found visiting Poland.

Is it expensive to buy things in Poland?

The good news is that Poland is relatively inexpensive in comparison to many other countries. You can actually buy many things in Poland with your money.

What kinds of food do people in Poland eat?

In Poland people eat all sorts of food. Some of the most popular dishes are meat and sauerkraut.

Which religion is practiced the most in Poland?

The religion which is practiced the most in Poland is Christianity.

How many years on average do the people in Poland live for?

The females live up until 82 years of age on average. The males live up until 74 years of age on average.

Is there a specific flower which is a national symbol of the country?

The answer is a big yes. The corn poppy is the name of the flower which is considered to be a national symbol of the country.

What type of landscape does Poland have?

Poland has a beautiful and scenic landscape. The country is surrounded by beaches, farms, forests and mountain ranges.

Is Poland well-known for anything?

You are too young to drink alcohol, so you won't know what it tastes like. With that being said, Poland is very well known for its vodka. Vodka is a very strong type of alcohol, which not everyone enjoys.

What goods do they usually export from the country?

Poland is known to export all different types of goods. The main goods include furniture, cars and car parts.

Which language do people speak in the country of Poland?

The main language which they speak in Poland is Polish. There are many other languages which they speak in the country too.

Which financial currency do they use in Poland?

If you wish to buy things in Poland, it may be useful for you to know which financial currency they use. The financial currency which they use in Poland is called the Polish Zloty.

Will you find any rivers in Poland?

The answer is a big yes. There are many rivers in Poland. The river which is most well-known is called the Vistula river. This is the longest river in the country.

What is the highest peak in the country called?

If you are looking for the highest peak in the country, you will find it at a spot called Rysy. This is the tallest peak in the country.

Will you find many animals in Poland?

If you love animals, you will be pleased to know that Poland is home to all sorts of different animals. If you look closely enough you may even find some unique animals that can only be found in Poland and nowhere else.

What is the population size of Poland?

Currently, there are over 40 million people living in the country of Poland. This amount increases each and every single year.

What type of weather do they experience in Poland?

The weather which they experience in Poland is usually quite cold. The country is known for being extremely cold during the winter months. It also is surprisingly warm during the summer months.

Is Poland a big or small country?

Poland is actually a very big country. It is one of the bigger countries which can be found in the world.

Is it safe to travel in Poland?

The good news is that Poland is a very safe country. The crime rate is very low and you should not experience any form of crime aside from the random petty theft.

What is the name of the capital city?

The name of the capital city is Warsaw. There are literally millions of people who live in this capital city.

Where in the world will you find Poland?

I am sure you have heard of a continent Europe? This is where you will find Poland.

Made in the USA
San Bernardino, CA
03 November 2019

59368568R00024